Lyrics Of Earth by Archibald Lampman

Archibald Lampman was born on November 17th 1861 at Morpeth, Ontario in Canada. Perhaps the finest Canadian Poet of his time he is classed as a Confederation Poet.

When he was 6 the family moved to Gore's Landing on Rice Lake, Ontario, where young Archie started school. In 1868 he contracted rheumatic fever, which left him lame for many years and with a permanently weakened heart.

He attended Trinity College School in Port Hope, Ontario, and then to Trinity College in Toronto, Ontario and graduated in 1882. Whilst there he published many poems in the literary journal of Victoria College.

After attempting a career as a teacher he became a clerk in the Post Office Department in Ottawa, a position he held for the rest of his life.

On Sep. 3, 1887, Arhibald married Maude Emma Playter. "They had three children; Natalie Charlotte in 1892. Arnold Gesner in May 1894, but he was only to survive a few months and in 1898 Archibald Otto, was born.

A lover of camping it inspired much of his verse and helped him to become known as 'The Canadian Keats'. Most of his poems are about the Countryside and the natural world. He wrote in excess of 300 poems and all reveal and revel in his observations of life and landscape.

But his life was destined to be cut short. His health deteriorated, due in part to the death of his second son and his earlier problems caused by rheumatic fever.

On February 10th, 1899 Archibald Lampman died of a weak heart, an after-effect of his childhood rheumatic fever in Ottawa at the age of only 37.

He is buried at Beechwood Cemetery, in Ottawa, His grave is marked by a single word on his headstone "Lampman.". A nearby plaque cites his poem "In November":
The hills grow wintry white, and bleak winds moan
About the naked uplands. I alone
Am neither sad, nor shelterless, nor gray
Wrapped round with thought, content to watch and dream.

Index Of Poems

TO MY MOTHER

Mother, to whose valiant will,
Battling long ago,
What the heaping years fulfil,
Light and song, I owe;
Send my little book a-field,
Fronting praise or blame
With the shining flag and shield
Of your name.

The Sweetness Of Life

It fell on a day I was happy,
And the winds, the concave sky,
The flowers and the beasts in the meadow
Seemed happy even as I;
And I stretched my hands to the meadow,
To the bird, the beast, the tree:
"Why are ye all so happy?"
I cried, and they answered me.

What sayest thou, Oh meadow,
That stretches so wide, so far,

That none can say how many
Thy misty marguerites are?
And what say ye, red roses,
That o'er the sun-blanched wall
From your high black-shadowed trellis
Like flame or blood-drops fall?
"We are born, we are reared, and we linger
A various space and die;
We dream, and are bright and happy,
But we cannot answer why."

What sayest thou, Oh shadow,
That from the dreaming hill
All down the broadening valley
Liest so sharp and still?
And thou, Oh murmuring brooklet,
Whereby in the noonday gleam
The loosestrife burns like ruby,
And the branchèd asters dream?
"We are born, we are reared, and we linger
A various space and die;
We dream and are very happy,
But we cannot answer why."

And then of myself I questioned,
That like a ghost the while
Stood from me and calmly answered,
With slow and curious smile:
"Thou art born as the flowers, and wilt linger
Thine own short space and die;
Thou dream'st and art strangely happy,
But thou canst not answer why."

God Speed To The Snow
March is slain; the keen winds fly;
Nothing more is thine to do;
April kisses thee good-bye;
Thou must haste and follow too;
Silent friend that guarded well
Withered things to make us glad,
Shyest friend that could not tell
Half the kindly thought he had.
Haste thee, speed thee, O kind snow;
Down the dripping valleys go,
From the fields and gleaming meadows,
Where the slaying hours behold thee,
From the forests whose slim shadows,
Brown and leafless cannot fold thee,
Through the cedar lands aflame
With gold light that cleaves and quivers,
Songs that winter may not tame,

Drone of pines and laugh of rivers.
May thy passing joyous be
To thy father, the great sea,
For the sun is getting stronger;
Earth hath need of thee no longer;
Go, kind snow, God-speed to thee!

April In The Hills

To-day the world is wide and fair
With sunny fields of lucid air,
And waters dancing everywhere;
The snow is almost gone;
The noon is builded high with light,
And over heaven's liquid height,
In steady fleets serene and white,
The happy clouds go on.

The channels run, the bare earth steams,
And every hollow rings and gleams
With jetting falls and dashing streams;
The rivers burst and fill;
The fields are full of little lakes,
And when the romping wind awakes
The water ruffles blue and shakes,
And the pines roar on the hill.

The crows go by, a noisy throng;
About the meadows all day long
The shore-lark drops his brittle song;
And up the leafless tree
The nut-hatch runs, and nods, and clings;
The bluebird dips with flashing wings,
The robin flutes, the sparrow sings,
And the swallows float and flee.

I break the spirit's cloudy bands,
A wanderer in enchanted lands,
I feel the sun upon my hands;
And far from care and strife
The broad earth bids me forth. I rise
With lifted brow and upward eyes.
I bathe my spirit in blue skies,
And taste the springs of life.

I feel the tumult of new birth;
I waken with the wakening earth;
I match the bluebird in her mirth;
And wild with wind and sun,
A treasurer of immortal days,
I roam the glorious world with praise,
The hillsides and the woodland ways,

Till earth and I are one.

Forest Moods

There is singing of birds in the deep wet woods,
In the heart of the listening solitudes,
Pewees, and thrushes, and sparrows, not few,
And all the notes of their throats are true.

The thrush from the innermost ash takes on
A tender dream of the treasured and gone;
But the sparrow singeth with pride and cheer
Of the might and light of the present and here.

There is shining of flowers in the deep wet woods,
In the heart of the sensitive solitudes,
The roseate bell and the lily are there,
And every leaf of their sheaf is fair.

Careless and bold, without dream of woe,
The trilliums scatter their flags snow;
But the pale wood-daffodil covers her face,
Agloom with the doom of a sorrowful race.

The Return Of The Year

Again the warm bare earth, the noon
That hangs upon her healing scars,
The midnight round, the great red moon,
The mother with her brood of stars,

The mist-rack and the wakening rain
Blown soft in many a forest way,
The yellowing elm-trees, and again
The blood-root in its sheath of gray.

The vesper-sparrow's song, the stress
Of yearning notes that gush and stream,
The lyric joy, the tenderness,
And once again the dream! the dream!

A touch of far-off joy and power,
A something it is life to learn,
Comes back to earth, and one short hour
The glamours of the gods return.

This life's old mood and cult of care
Falls smitten by an older truth,
And the gray world wins back to her
The rapture of her vanished youth.

Dead thoughts revive, and he that heeds

Shall hear, as by a spirit led,
A song among the golden reeds:
"The gods are vanished but not dead!"

For one short hour; unseen yet near,
They haunt us, a forgotten mood,
A glory upon mead and mere,
A magic in the leafless wood.

At morning we shall catch the glow
Of Dian's quiver on the hill,
And somewhere in the glades I know
That Pan is at his piping still.

Favorites Of Pan
Once, long ago, before the gods
Had left this earth, by stream and forest glade,
Where the first plough upturned the clinging sods,
Or the lost shepherd strayed,

Often to the tired listener's ear
There came at noonday or beneath the stars
A sound, he knew not whence, so sweet and clear,
That all his aches and scars

And every brooded bitterness,
Fallen asunder from his soul took flight,
Like mist or darkness yielding to the press
Of an unnamed delight,

A sudden brightness of the heart,
A magic fire drawn down from Paradise,
That rent the cloud with golden gleam apart,
And far before his eyes

The loveliness and calm of earth
Lay like a limitless dream remote and strange,
The joy, the strife, the triumph and the mirth,
And the enchanted change;

And so he followed the sweet sound,
Till faith had traversed her appointed span,
And murmured as he pressed the sacred ground:
"It is the note of Pan!"

Now though no more by marsh or stream
Or dewy forest sounds the secret reed
For Pan is gone. Ah yet, the infinite dream
Still lives for them that heed.

In April, when the turning year

Regains its pensive youth, and a soft breath
And amorous influence over marsh and mere
Dissolves the grasp of death,

To them that are in love with life,
Wandering like children with untroubled eyes,
Far from the noise of cities and the strife,
Strange flute-like voices rise

At noon and in the quiet of the night
From every watery waste; and in that hour
The same strange spell, the same unnamed delight,
Enfolds them in its power.

An old-world joyousness supreme,
The warmth and glow of an immortal balm,
The mood-touch of the gods, the endless dream,
The high lethean calm.

They see, wide on the eternal way,
The services of earth, the life of man;
And, listening to the magic cry they say:
"It is the note of Pan!"

For, long ago, when the new strains
Of hostile hymns and conquering faiths grew keen,
And the old gods from their deserted fanes,
Fled silent and unseen,

So, too, the goat-foot Pan, not less
Sadly obedient to the mightier hand,
Cut him new reeds, and in a sore distress
Passed out from land to land;

And lingering by each haunt he knew,
Of fount or sinuous stream or grassy marge,
He set the syrinx to his lips, and blew
A note divinely large;

And all around him on the wet
Cool earth the frogs came up, and with a smile
He took them in his hairy hands, and set
His mouth to theirs awhile,

And blew into their velvet throats;
And ever from that hour the frogs repeat
The murmur of Pan's pipes, the notes,
And answers strange and sweet;

And they that hear them are renewed
By knowledge in some god-like touch conveyed,
Entering again into the eternal mood,

Wherein the world was made.

The Meadow
Here when the cloudless April days begin,
And the quaint crows flock thicker day by day,
Filling the forests with a pleasant din,
And the soiled snow creeps secretly away,
Comes the small busy sparrow, primed with glee,
First preacher in the naked wilderness,
Piping an end to all the long distress
From every fence and every leafless tree.

Now with soft slight and viewless artifice
Winter's iron work is wondrously undone;
In all the little hollows cored with ice
The clear brown pools stand simmering in the sun,
Frail lucid worlds, upon whose tremulous floors
All day the wandering water-bugs at will,
Shy mariners whose oars are never still,
Voyage and dream about the heightening shores.

The bluebird, peeping from the gnarlèd thorn,
Prattles upon his frolic flute, or flings,
In bounding flight across the golden morn,
An azure gleam from off his splendid wings.
Here the slim-pinioned swallows sweep and pass
Down to the far-off river; the black crow
With wise and wary visage to and fro
Settles and stalks about the withered grass.

Here, when the murmurous May-day is half gone,
The watchful lark before my feet takes flight,
And wheeling to some lonelier field far on,
Drops with obstreperous cry; and here at night,
When the first star precedes the great red moon,
The shore-lark tinkles from the darkening field,
Somewhere, we know not, in the dusk concealed,
His little creakling and continuous tune.

Here, too, the robins, lusty as of old,
Hunt the waste grass for forage, or prolong
From every quarter of these fields the bold,
Blithe phrases of their never-finished song.
The white-throat's distant descant with slow stress
Note after note upon the noonday falls,
Filling the leisured air at intervals
With his own mood of piercing pensiveness.

How often from this windy upland perch,
Mine eyes have seen the forest break in bloom,
The rose-red maple and the golden birch,

The dusty yellow of the elms, the gloom
Of the tall poplar hung with tasseled black;
Ah, I have watched, till eye and ear and brain
Grew full of dreams as they, the moted plain,
The sun-steeped wood, the marsh-land at its back,

The valley where the river wheels and fills,
Yon city glimmering in its smoky shroud,
And out at the last misty rim the hills
Blue and far off and mounded like a cloud,
And here the noisy rutted road that goes
Down the slope yonder, flanked on either side
With the smooth-furrowed fields flung black and wide,
Patched with pale water sleeping in the rows.

So as I watched the crowded leaves expand,
The bloom break sheath, the summer's strength uprear,
In earth's great mother's heart already planned
The heaped and burgeoned plenty of the year,
Even as she from out her wintry cell
My spirit also sprang to life anew,
And day by day as the spring's bounty grew,
Its conquering joy possessed me like a spell.

In reverie by day and midnight dream
I sought these upland fields and walked apart,
Musing on Nature, till my thought did seem
To read the very secrets of her heart;
In mooded moments earnest and sublime
I stored the themes of many a future song,
Whose substance should be Nature's, clear and strong,
Bound in a casket of majestic rhyme.

Brave bud-like plans that never reached the fruit,
Like hers our mother's who with every hour,
Easily replenished from the sleepless root,
Covers her bosom with fresh bud and flower;
Yet I was happy as young lovers be,
Who in the season of their passion's birth
Deem that they have their utmost worship's worth,
If love be near them, just to hear and see.

In May
Grief was my master yesternight;
To-morrow I may grieve again;
But now along the windy plain
The clouds have taken flight.

The sowers in the furrows go;
The lusty river brimmeth on;
The curtains from the hills are gone;

The leaves are out; and lo,

The silvery distance of the day,
The light horizons, and between
The glory of the perfect green,
The tumult of the May.

The bobolinks at noonday sing
More softly than the softest flute,
And lightlier than the lightest lute
Their fairy tambours ring.

The roads far off are towered with dust;
The cherry-blooms are swept and thinned;
In yonder swaying elms the wind
Is charging gust on gust.

But here there is no stir at all;
The ministers of sun and shadow
Horde all the perfumes of the meadow
Behind a grassy wall.

An infant rivulet wind-free
Adown the guarded hollow sets,
Over whose brink the violets
Are nodding peacefully.

From pool to pool it prattles by;
The flashing swallows dip and pass,
Above the tufted marish grass,
And here at rest am I.

I care not for the old distress,
Nor if to-morrow bid me moan;
To-day is mine, and I have known
An hour of blessedness.

Life And Nature

I passed through the gates of the city,
The streets were strange and still,
Through the doors of the open churches
The organs were moaning shrill.

Through the doors and the great high windows
I heard the murmur of prayer,
And the sound of their solemn singing
Streamed out on the sunlit air;

A sound of some great burden
That lay on the world's dark breast,
Of the old, and the sick, and the lonely,

And the weary that cried for rest.

I strayed through the midst of the city
Like one distracted or mad.
"Oh, Life! Oh, Life!" I kept saying,
And the very word seemed sad.

I passed through the gates of the city,
And I heard the small birds sing,
I laid me down in the meadows
Afar from the bell-ringing.

In the depth and the bloom of the meadows
I lay on the earth's quiet breast,
The poplar fanned me with shadows,
And the veery sang me to rest.

Blue, blue was the heaven above me,
And the earth green at my feet;
"Oh, Life! Oh, Life!" I kept saying,
And the very word seemed sweet.

With The Night

O doubts, dull passions, and base fears,
That harassed and oppressed the day,
Ye poor remorses and vain tears,
That shook this house of clay:

All heaven to the western bars
Is glittering with the darker dawn;
Here with the earth, the night, the stars,
Ye have no place: begone!

June

Long, long ago, it seems, this summer morn
That pale-browed April passed with pensive tread
Through the frore woods, and from its frost-bound bed
Woke the arbutus with her silver horn;
And now May, too, is fled,
The flower-crowned month, the merry laughing May,
With rosy feet and fingers dewy wet,
Leaving the woods and all cool gardens gay
With tulips and the scented violet.

Gone are the wind-flower and the adder-tongue
And the sad drooping bellwort, and no more
The snowy trilliums crowd the forest's floor;
The purpling grasses are no longer young,
And summer's wide-set door
O'er the thronged hills and the broad panting earth

Lets in the torrent of the later bloom,
Haytime, and harvest, and the after mirth,
The slow soft rain, the rushing thunder plume.

All day in garden alleys moist and dim,
The humid air is burdened with the rose;
In moss-deep woods the creamy orchid blows;
And now the vesper-sparrows' pealing hymn
From every orchard close
At eve comes flooding rich and silvery;
The daisies in great meadows swing and shine;
And with the wind a sound as of the sea
Roars in the maples and the topmost pine.

High in the hills the solitary thrush
Tunes magically his music of fine dreams,
In briary dells, by boulder-broken streams;
And wide and far on nebulous fields aflush
The mellow morning gleams.
The orange cone-flowers purple-bossed are there,
The meadow's bold-eyed gypsies deep of hue,
And slender hawkweed tall and softly fair,
And rosy tops of fleabane veiled with dew.

So with thronged voices and unhasting flight
The fervid hours with long return go by;
The far-heard hylas piping shrill and high
Tell the slow moments of the solemn night
With unremitting cry;
Lustrous and large out of the gathering drouth
The planets gleam; the baleful Scorpion
Trails his dim fires along the droused south;
The silent world-incrusted round moves on.

And all the dim night long the moon's white beams
Nestle deep down in every brooding tree,
And sleeping birds, touched with a silly glee,
Waken at midnight from their blissful dreams,
And carol brokenly.
Dim surging motions and uneasy dreads
Scare the light slumber from men's busy eyes,
And parted lovers on their restless beds
Toss and yearn out, and cannot sleep for sighs.

Oft have I striven, sweet month, to figure thee,
As dreamers of old time were wont to feign,
In living form of flesh, and striven in vain;
Yet when some sudden old-world mystery
Of passion fired my brain,
Thy shape hath flashed upon me like no dream,
Wandering with scented curls that heaped the breeze,
Or by the hollow of some reeded stream

Sitting waist-deep in white anemones;

And even as I glimpsed thee thou wert gone,
A dream for mortal eyes too proudly coy,
Yet in thy place for subtle thought's employ
The golden magic clung, a light that shone
And filled me with thy joy.
Before me like a mist that streamed and fell
All names and shapes of antique beauty passed
In garlanded procession with the swell
Of flutes between the beechen stems; and last,

I saw the Arcadian valley, the loved wood,
Alpheus stream divine, the sighing shore,
And through the cool green glades, awake once more,
Psyche, the white-limbed goddess, still pursued,
Fleet-footed as of yore,
The noonday ringing with her frighted peals,
Down the bright sward and through the reeds she ran,
Urged by the mountain echoes, at her heels
The hot-blown cheeks and trampling feet of Pan.

Distance
To the distance! Ah, the distance!
Blue and broad and dim!
Peace is not in burgh or meadow,
But beyond the rim.

Aye, beyond it, far beyond it;
Follow still my soul,
Till this earth is lost in heaven,
And thou feel'st the whole.

The Bird And The Hour
The sun looks over a little hill
And floods the valley with gold
A torrent of gold;
And the hither field is green and still;
Beyond it a cloud outrolled,
Is glowing molten and bright;
And soon the hill, and the valley and all,
With a quiet fall,
Shall be gathered into the night.
And yet a moment more,
Out of the silent wood,
As if from the closing door
Of another world and another lovelier mood,
Hear'st thou the hermit pour
So sweet! so magical!
His golden music, ghostly beautiful.

After Rain

For three whole days across the sky,
In sullen packs that loomed and broke,
With flying fringes dim as smoke,
The columns of the rain went by;
At every hour the wind awoke;
The darkness passed upon the plain;
The great drops rattled at the pane.

Now piped the wind, or far aloof
Fell to a sough remote and dull;
And all night long with rush and lull
The rain kept drumming on the roof:
I heard till ear and sense were full
The clash or silence of the leaves,
The gurgle in the creaking eaves.

But when the fourth day came at noon,
The darkness and the rain were by;
The sunward roofs were steaming dry;
And all the world was flecked and strewn
With shadows from a fleecy sky.
The haymakers were forth and gone,
And every rillet laughed and shone.

Then, too, on me that loved so well
The world, despairing in her blight,
Uplifted with her least delight,
On me, as on the earth, there fell
New happiness of mirth and might;
I strode the valleys pied and still;
I climbed upon the breezy hill.

I watched the gray hawk wheel and drop,
Sole shadow on the shining world;
I saw the mountains clothed and curled,
With forest ruffling to the top;
I saw the river's length unfurled,
Pale silver down the fruited plain,
Grown great and stately with the rain.

Through miles of shadow and soft heat,
Where field and fallow, fence and tree,
Were all one world of greenery,
I heard the robin ringing sweet,
The sparrow piping silverly,
The thrushes at the forest's hem;
And as I went I sang with them.

Cloud Break

With a turn of his magical rod,
That extended and suddenly shone,
From the round of his glory some god
Looks forth and is gone.

To the summit of heaven the clouds
Are rolling aloft like steam;
There's a break in their infinite shrouds,
And below it a gleam.
O'er the drift of the river a whiff
Comes out from the blossoming shore;
And the meadows are greening, as if
They never were green before.

The islands are kindled with gold
And russet and emerald dye;
And the interval waters outrolled
Are more blue than the sky.
From my feet to the heart of the hills
The spirits of May intervene,
And a vapor of azure distills
Like a breath on the opaline green.

Only a moment! and then
The chill and the shadow decline,
On the eyes of rejuvenate men
That were wide and divine.

The Moon Path

The full, clear moon uprose and spread
Her cold, pale splendor o'er the sea;
A light-strewn path that seemed to lead
Outward into eternity.
Between the darkness and the gleam
An old-world spell encompassed me:
Methought that in a godlike dream
I trod upon the sea.

And lo! upon that glimmering road,
In shining companies unfurled,
The trains of many a primal god,
The monsters of the elder world;
Strange creatures that, with silver wings,
Scarce touched the ocean's thronging floor,
The phantoms of old tales, and things
Whose shapes are known no more.

Giants and demi-gods who once
Were dwellers of the earth and sea,
And they who from Deucalion's stones,

Rose men without an infancy;
Beings on whose majestic lids
Time's solemn secrets seemed to dwell,
Tritons and pale-limbed Nereids,
And forms of heaven and hell.

Some who were heroes long of yore,
When the great world was hale and young;
And some whose marble lips yet pour
The murmur of an antique tongue;
Sad queens, whose names are like soft moans,
Whose griefs were written up in gold;
And some who on their silver thrones
Were goddesses of old.

As if I had been dead indeed,
And come into some after-land,
I saw them pass me, and take heed,
And touch me with each mighty hand;
And evermore a murmurous stream,
So beautiful they seemed to me,
Not less than in a godlike dream
I trod the shining sea.

Comfort Of The Fields
What would'st thou have for easement after grief,
When the rude world hath used thee with despite,
And care sits at thine elbow day and night,
Filching thy pleasures like a subtle thief?
To me, when life besets me in such wise,
'Tis sweetest to break forth, to drop the chain,
And grasp the freedom of this pleasant earth,
To roam in idleness and sober mirth,
Through summer airs and summer lands, and drain
The comfort of wide fields unto tired eyes.

By hills and waters, farms and solitudes,
To wander by the day with wilful feet;
Through fielded valleys wide with yellowing wheat;
Along gray roads that run between deep woods,
Murmurous and cool; through hallowed slopes of pine,
Where the long daylight dreams, unpierced, unstirred,
And only the rich-throated thrush is heard;
By lonely forest brooks that froth and shine
In bouldered crannies buried in the hills;
By broken beeches tangled with wild vine,
And log-strewn rivers murmurous with mills.

In upland pastures, sown with gold, and sweet
With the keen perfume of the ripening grass,
Where wings of birds and filmy shadows pass,

Spread thick as stars with shining marguerite;
To haunt old fences overgrown with brier,
Muffled in vines, and hawthorns, and wild cherries,
Rank poisonous ivies, red-bunched elderberries,
And pièd blossoms to the heart's desire,
Gray mullein towering into yellow bloom,
Pink-tasseled milkweed, breathing dense perfume,
And swarthy vervain, tipped with violet fire.

To hear at eve the bleating of far flocks,
The mud-hen's whistle from the marsh at morn;
To skirt with deafened ears and brain o'erborne
Some foam-filled rapid charging down its rocks
With iron roar of waters; far away
Across wide-reeded meres, pensive with noon,
To hear the querulous outcry of the loon;
To lie among deep rocks, and watch all day
On liquid heights the snowy clouds melt by;
Or hear from wood-capped mountain-brows the jay
Pierce the bright morning with his jibing cry.

To feast on summer sounds; the jolted wains,
The thrasher humming from the farm near by,
The prattling cricket's intermittent cry,
The locust's rattle from the sultry lanes;
Or in the shadow of some oaken spray,
To watch, as through a mist of light and dreams,
The far-off hay-fields, where the dusty teams
Drive round and round the lessening squares of hay,
And hear upon the wind, now loud, now low,
With drowsy cadence half a summer's day,
The clatter of the reapers come and go.

Far violet hills, horizons filmed with showers,
The murmur of cool streams, the forest's gloom,
The voices of the breathing grass, the hum
Of ancient gardens overbanked with flowers:
Thus, with a smile as golden as the dawn,
And cool fair fingers radiantly divine,
The mighty mother brings us in her hand,
For all tired eyes and foreheads pinched and wan,
Her restful cup, her beaker of bright wine:
Drink, and be filled, and ye shall understand!

At The Ferry
On such a day the shrunken stream
Spends its last water and runs dry;
Clouds like far turrets in a dream
Stand baseless in the burning sky.
On such a day at every rod
The toilers in the hay-field halt,

With dripping brows, and the parched sod
Yields to the crushing foot like salt.

But here a little wind astir,
Seen waterward in jetting lines,
From yonder hillside topped with fir
Comes pungent with the breath of pines;
And here when all the noon hangs still,
White-hot upon the city tiles,
A perfume and a wintry chill
Breathe from the yellow lumber-piles.

And all day long there falls a blur
Of noises upon listless ears,
The rumble of the trams, the stir
Of barges at the clacking piers;
The champ of wheels, the crash of steam,
And ever, without change or stay,
The drone, as through a troubled dream,
Of waters falling far away.

A tug-boat up the farther shore
Half pants, half whistles, in her draught;
The cadence of a creaking oar
Falls drowsily; a corded raft
Creeps slowly in the noonday gleam,
And wheresoe'er a shadow sleeps
The men lie by, or half a-dream,
Stand leaning at the idle sweeps.

And all day long in the quiet bay
The eddying amber depths retard,
And hold, as in a ring, at play,
The heavy saw-logs notched and scarred;
And yonder between cape and shoal,
Where the long currents swing and shift,
An aged punt-man with his pole
Is searching in the parted drift.

At moments from the distant glare
The murmur of a railway steals
Round yonder jutting point the air
Is beaten with the puff of wheels;
And here at hand an open mill,
Strong clamor at perpetual drive,
With changing chant, now hoarse, now shrill,
Keeps dinning like a mighty hive.

A furnace over field and mead,
The rounding noon hangs hard and white;
Into the gathering heats recede
The hollows of the Chelsea height;

But under all to one quiet tune,
A spirit in cool depths withdrawn,
With logs, and dust, and wrack bestrewn,
The stately river journeys on.

I watch the swinging currents go
Far down to where, enclosed and piled,
The logs crowd, and the Gatineau
Comes rushing from the northern wild.
I see the long low point, where close
The shore-lines, and the waters end,
I watch the barges pass in rows
That vanish at the tapering bend.

I see as at the noon's pale core
A shadow that lifts clear and floats
The cabin'd village round the shore,
The landing and the fringe of boats;
Faint films of smoke that curl and wreathe,
And upward with the like desire
The vast gray church that seems to breathe
In heaven with its dreaming spire.

And there the last blue boundaries rise,
That guard within their compass furled
This plot of earth: beyond them lies
The mystery of the echoing world;
And still my thought goes on, and yields
New vision and new joy to me,
Far peopled hills, and ancient fields,
And cities by the crested sea.

I see no more the barges pass,
Nor mark the ripple round the pier,
And all the uproar, mass on mass,
Falls dead upon a vacant ear.
Beyond the tumult of the mills,
And all the city's sound and strife,
Beyond the waste, beyond the hills,
I look far out and dream of life.

September
Now hath the summer reached her golden close,
And, lost amid her corn-fields, bright of soul,
Scarcely perceives from her divine repose
How near, how swift, the inevitable goal:
Still, still, she smiles, though from her careless feet
The bounty and the fruitful strength are gone,
And through the soft long wondering days goes on
The silent sere decadence sad and sweet.

The kingbird and the pensive thrush are fled,
Children of light, too fearful of the gloom;
The sun falls low, the secret word is said,
The mouldering woods grow silent as the tomb;
Even the fields have lost their sovereign grace,
The cone-flower and the marguerite; and no more,
Across the river's shadow-haunted floor,
The paths of skimming swallows interlace.

Already in the outland wilderness
The forests echo with unwonted dins;
In clamorous gangs the gathering woodmen press
Northward, and the stern winter's toil begins.
Around the long low shanties, whose rough lines
Break the sealed dreams of many an unnamed lake,
Already in the frost-clear morns awake
The crash and thunder of the falling pines.

Where the tilled earth, with all its fields set free,
Naked and yellow from the harvest lies,
By many a loft and busy granary,
The hum and tumult of the thrashers rise;
There the tanned farmers labor without slack,
Till twilight deepens round the spouting mill,
Feeding the loosened sheaves, or with fierce will,
Pitching waist-deep upon the dusty stack.

Still a brief while, ere the old year quite pass,
Our wandering steps and wistful eyes shall greet
The leaf, the water, the beloved grass;
Still from these haunts and this accustomed seat
I see the wood-wrapt city, swept with light,
The blue long-shadowed distance, and, between,
The dotted farm-lands with their parcelled green,
The dark pine forest and the watchful height.

I see the broad rough meadow stretched away
Into the crystal sunshine, wastes of sod,
Acres of withered vervain, purple-gray,
Branches of aster, groves of goldenrod;
And yonder, toward the sunlit summit, strewn
With shadowy boulders, crowned and swathed with weed,
Stand ranks of silken thistles, blown to seed,
Long silver fleeces shining like the noon.

In far-off russet corn-fields, where the dry
Gray shocks stand peaked and withering, half concealed
In the rough earth, the orange pumpkins lie,
Full-ribbed; and in the windless pasture-field
The sleek red horses o'er the sun-warmed ground
Stand pensively about in companies,
While all around them from the motionless trees

The long clean shadows sleep without a sound.

Under cool elm-trees floats the distant stream,
Moveless as air; and o'er the vast warm earth
The fathomless daylight seems to stand and dream,
A liquid cool elixir all its girth
Bound with faint haze, a frail transparency,
Whose lucid purple barely veils and fills
The utmost valleys and the thin last hills,
Nor mars one whit their perfect clarity.

Thus without grief the golden days go by,
So soft we scarcely notice how they wend,
And like a smile half happy, or a sigh,
The summer passes to her quiet end;
And soon, too soon, around the cumbered eaves
Sly frosts shall take the creepers by surprise,
And through the wind-touched reddening woods shall rise
October with the rain of ruined leaves.

A Re-Assurance
With what doubting eyes, oh sparrow,
Thou regardest me,
Underneath yon spray of yarrow,
Dipping cautiously.

Fear me not, oh little sparrow,
Bathe and never fear,
For to me both pool and yarrow
And thyself are dear.

The Poet's Possession
Think not, oh master of the well-tilled field,
This earth is only thine; for after thee,
When all is sown and gathered and put by,
Comes the grave poet with creative eye,
And from these silent acres and clean plots,
Bids with his wand the fancied after-yield,
A second tilth and second harvest, be,
The crop of images and curious thoughts.

An Autumn Landscape
No wind there is that either pipes or moans;
The fields are cold and still; the sky
Is covered with a blue-gray sheet
Of motionless cloud; and at my feet
The river, curling softly by,
Whispers and dimples round its quiet gray stones.

Along the chill green slope that dips and heaves
The road runs rough and silent, lined
With plum-trees, misty and blue-gray,
And poplars pallid as the day,
In masses spectral, undefined,
Pale greenish stems half hid in dry gray leaves.

And on beside the river's sober edge
A long fresh field lies black. Beyond,
Low thickets gray and reddish stand,
Stroked white with birch; and near at hand,
Over a little steel-smooth pond,
Hang multitudes of thin and withering sedge.

Across a waste and solitary rise
A ploughman urges his dull team,
A stooped gray figure with prone brow
That plunges bending to the plough
With strong, uneven steps. The stream
Rings and re-echoes with his furious cries.

Sometimes the lowing of a cow, long-drawn,
Comes from far off; and crows in strings
Pass on the upper silences.
A flock of small gray goldfinches,
Flown down with silvery twitterings,
Rustle among the birch-cones and are gone.

This day the season seems like one that heeds,
With fixèd ear and lifted hand,
All moods that yet are known on earth,
All motions that have faintest birth,
If haply she may understand
The utmost inward sense of all her deeds.

In November
With loitering step and quiet eye,
Beneath the low November sky,
I wandered in the woods, and found
A clearing, where the broken ground
Was scattered with black stumps and briers,
And the old wreck of forest fires.
It was a bleak and sandy spot,
And, all about, the vacant plot
Was peopled and inhabited
By scores of mulleins long since dead.
A silent and forsaken brood
In that mute opening of the wood,
So shrivelled and so thin they were,
So gray, so haggard, and austere,
Not plants at all they seemed to me,

But rather some spare company
Of hermit folk, who long ago,
Wandering in bodies to and fro,
Had chanced upon this lonely way,
And rested thus, till death one day
Surprised them at their compline prayer,
And left them standing lifeless there.

There was no sound about the wood
Save the wind's secret stir. I stood
Among the mullein-stalks as still
As if myself had grown to be
One of their sombre company,
A body without wish or will.
And as I stood, quite suddenly,
Down from a furrow in the sky
The sun shone out a little space
Across that silent sober place,
Over the sand heaps and brown sod,
The mulleins and dead goldenrod,
And passed beyond the thickets gray,
And lit the fallen leaves that lay,
Level and deep within the wood,
A rustling yellow multitude.

And all around me the thin light,
So sere, so melancholy bright,
Fell like the half-reflected gleam
Or shadow of some former dream;
A moment's golden revery
Poured out on every plant and tree
A semblance of weird joy, or less,
A sort of spectral happiness;
And I, too, standing idly there,
With muffled hands in the chill air,
Felt the warm glow about my feet,
And shuddering betwixt cold and heat,
Drew my thoughts closer, like a cloak,
While something in my blood awoke,
A nameless and unnatural cheer,
A pleasure secret and austere.

By An Autumn Stream
Now overhead,
Where the rivulet loiters and stops,
The bittersweet hangs from the tops
Of the alders and cherries
Its bunches of beautiful berries,
Orange and red.

And the snowbirds flee,

Tossing up on the far brown field,
Now flashing and now concealed,
Like fringes of spray
That vanish and gleam on the gray
Field of the sea.

Flickering light,
Come the last of the leaves down borne,
And patches of pale white corn
In the wind complain,
Like the slow rustle of rain
Noticed by night.

Withered and thinned,
The sentinel mullein looms,
With the pale gray shadowy plumes
Of the goldenrod;
And the milkweed opens its pod,
Tempting the wind.

Aloft on the hill,
A cloudrift opens and shines
Through a break in its gorget of pines,
And it dreams at my feet
In a sad, silvery sheet,
Utterly still.

All things that be
Seem plunged into silence, distraught,
By some stern, some necessitous thought:
It wraps and enthralls
Marsh, meadow, and forest; and falls
Also on me.

Snowbirds
Along the narrow sandy height
I watch them swiftly come and go,
Or round the leafless wood,
Like flurries of wind-driven snow,
Revolving in perpetual flight,
A changing multitude.

Nearer and nearer still they sway,
And, scattering in a circled sweep,
Rush down without a sound;
And now I see them peer and peep,
Across yon level bleak and gray,
Searching the frozen ground,

Until a little wind upheaves,
And makes a sudden rustling there,

And then they drop their play,
Flash up into the sunless air,
And like a flight of silver leaves
Swirl round and sweep away.

Snow

White are the far-off plains, and white
The fading forests grow;
The wind dies out along the height,
And denser still the snow,
A gathering weight on roof and tree,
Falls down scarce audibly.

The road before me smooths and fills
Apace, and all about
The fences dwindle, and the hills
Are blotted slowly out;
The naked trees loom spectrally
Into the dim white sky.

The meadows and far-sheeted streams
Lie still without a sound;
Like some soft minister of dreams
The snow-fall hoods me round;
In wood and water, earth and air,
A silence everywhere.

Save when at lonely intervals
Some farmer's sleigh, urged on,
With rustling runners and sharp bells,
Swings by me and is gone;
Or from the empty waste I hear
A sound remote and clear;

The barking of a dog, or call
To cattle, sharply pealed,
Borne echoing from some wayside stall
Or barnyard far a-field;
Then all is silent, and the snow
Falls, settling soft and slow.

The evening deepens, and the gray
Folds closer earth and sky;
The world seems shrouded far away;
Its noises sleep, and I,
As secret as yon buried stream,
Plod dumbly on, and dream.

Sunset

From this windy bridge at rest,

In some former curious hour,
We have watched the city's hue,
All along the orange west,
Cupola and pointed tower,
Darken into solid blue.

Tho' the biting north wind breaks
Full across this drifted hold,
Let us stand with icèd cheeks
Watching westward as of old;

Past the violet mountain-head
To the farthest fringe of pine,
Where far off the purple-red
Narrows to a dusky line,
And the last pale splendors die
Slowly from the olive sky;

Till the thin clouds wear away
Into threads of purple-gray,
And the sudden stars between
Brighten in the pallid green;

Till above the spacious east,
Slow returnèd one by one,
Like pale prisoners released
From the dungeons of the sun,
Capella and her train appear
In the glittering Charioteer;

Till the rounded moon shall grow
Great above the eastern snow,
Shining into burnished gold;
And the silver earth outrolled,
In the misty yellow light,
Shall take on the width of night.

Winter Store
Subtly conscious, all awake,
Let us clear our eyes, and break
Through the cloudy chrysalis,
See the wonder as it is.
Down a narrow alley, blind,
Touch and vision, heart and mind;
Turned sharply inward, still we plod,
Till the calmly smiling god
Leaves us, and our spirits grow
More thin, more acrid, as we go.
Creeping by the sullen wall,
We forego the power to see,
The threads that bind us to the All,

God or the Immensity;
Whereof on the eternal road
Man is but a passing mode.

Too blind we are, too little see
Of the magic pageantry,
Every minute, every hour,
From the cloudflake to the flower,
Forever old, forever strange,
Issuing in perpetual change
From the rainbow gates of Time.

But he who through this common air
Surely knows the great and fair,
What is lovely, what sublime,
Becomes in an increasing span,
One with earth and one with man,
One, despite these mortal scars,
With the planets and the stars;
And Nature from her holy place,
Bending with unveilèd face,
Fills him in her divine employ
With her own majestic joy.

Up the fielded slopes at morn,
Where light wefts of shadow pass,
Films upon the bending corn,
I shall sweep the purple grass.
Sun-crowned heights and mossy woods,
And the outer solitudes,
Mountain-valleys, dim with pine,
Shall be home and haunt of mine.
I shall search in crannied hollows,
Where the sunlight scarcely follows,
And the secret forest brook
Murmurs, and from nook to nook
Forever downward curls and cools,
Frothing in the bouldered pools.

Many a noon shall find me laid
In the pungent balsam shade,
Where sharp breezes spring and shiver
On some deep rough-coasted river,
And the plangent waters come,
Amber-hued and streaked with foam;
Where beneath the sunburnt hills
All day long the crowded mills
With remorseless champ and scream
Overlord the sluicing stream,
And the rapids' iron roar
Hammers at the forest's core;
Where corded rafts creep slowly on,

Glittering in the noonday sun,
And the tawny river-dogs,
Shepherding the branded logs,
Bind and heave with cadenced cry;
Where the blackened tugs go by,
Panting hard and straining slow,
Laboring at the weighty tow,
Flat-nosed barges all in trim,
Creeping in long cumbrous line,
Loaded to the water's brim
With the clean, cool-scented pine.

Perhaps in some low meadow-land,
Stretching wide on either hand,
I shall see the belted bees
Rocking with the tricksy breeze
In the spirèd meadow-sweet,
Or with eager trampling feet
Burrowing in the boneset blooms,
Treading out the dry perfumes.
Where sun-hot hay-fields newly mown
Climb the hillside ruddy brown,
I shall see the haymakers,
While the noonday scarcely stirs,
Brown of neck and booted gray,
Tossing up the rustling hay,
While the hay-racks bend and rock,
As they take each scented cock,
Jolting over dip and rise;
And the wavering butterflies
O'er the spaces brown and bare
Light and wander here and there.

I shall stray by many a stream,
Where the half-shut lilies gleam.
Napping out the sultry days
In the quiet secluded bays;
Where the tasseled rushes tower,
O'er the purple pickerel-flower.
And the floating dragon-fly
Azure glint and crystal gleam
Watches o'er the burnished stream
With his eye of ebony;
Where the bull-frog lolls at rest
On his float of lily-leaves,
That the swaying water weaves,
And distends his yellow breast,
Lowing out from shore to shore
With a hollow vibrant roar;
Where the softest wind that blows
As it lightly comes and goes,
O'er the jungled river meads,

Stirs a whisper in the reeds,
And wakes the crowded bull-rushes
From their stately reveries,
Flashing through their long-leaved hordes
Like a brandishing of swords;
There, too, the frost-like arrow-flowers
Tremble to the golden core,
Children of enchanted hours,
Whom the rustling river bore
In the night's bewildered noon,
Woven of water and the moon.

I shall hear the grasshoppers
From the parched grass rehearse,
And with drowsy note prolong
Evermore the same thin song.
I shall hear the crickets tell
Stories by the humming well,
And mark the locust, with quaint eyes,
Caper in his cloak of gray
Like a jester in disguise
Rattling by the dusty way.

I shall dream by upland fences,
Where the season's wealth condenses
Over many a weedy wreck,
Wild, uncared-for, desert places,
That sovereign Beauty loves to deck
With her softest, dearest graces.
There the long year dreams in quiet,
And the summer's strength runs riot.
Shall I not remember these,
Deep in winter reveries?
Berried brier and thistle-bloom,
And milkweed with its dense perfume;
Slender vervain towering up
In a many-branchèd cup,
Like a candlestick, each spire
Kindled with a violet fire;
Matted creepers and wild cherries,
Purple-bunchèd elderberries,
And on scanty plots of sod
Groves of branchy goldenrod.

What though autumn mornings now,
Winterward with glittering brow,
Stiffen in the silver grass;
And what though robins flock and pass,
With subdued and sober call,
To the old year's funeral;
Though October's crimson leaves
Rustle at the gusty door,

And the tempest round the eaves
Alternate with pipe and roar;
I sit, as erst, unharmed, secure,
Conscious that my store is sure,
Whatsoe'er the fencèd fields,
Or the untilled forest yields
Of unhurt remembrances,
Or thoughts, far-glimpsed, half-followed, these
I have reaped and laid away,
A treasure of unwinnowed grain,
To the garner packed and gray
Gathered without toil or strain.

And when the darker days shall come,
And the fields are white and dumb;
When our fires are half in vain,
And the crystal starlight weaves
Mockeries of summer leaves,
Pictured on the icy pane;
When the high aurora gleams
Far above the Arctic streams
Like a line of shifting spears,
And the broad pine-circled meres,
Glimmering in that spectral light,
Thunder through the northern night;
Then within the bolted door
I shall con my summer store;
Though the fences scarcely show
Black above the drifted snow,
Though the icy sweeping wind
Whistle in the empty tree,
Safe within the sheltered mind,
I shall feed on memory.

Yet across the windy night
Comes upon its wings a cry;
Fashioned forms and modes take flight,
And a vision sad and high
Of the laboring world down there,
Where the lights burn red and warm,
Pricks my soul with sudden stare,
Glowing through the veils of storm.
In the city yonder sleep
Those who smile and those who weep,
Those whose lips are set with care,
Those whose brows are smooth and fair;
Mourners whom the dawning light
Shall grapple with an old distress;
Lovers folded at midnight
In their bridal happiness;
Pale watchers by belovèd beds,
Fallen a-drowse with nodding heads,

Whom sleep captured by surprise,
With the circles round their eyes;
Maidens with quiet-taken breath,
Dreaming of enchanted bowers;
Old men with the mask of death;
Little children soft as flowers;
Those who wake wild-eyed and start
In some madness of the heart;
Those whose lips and brows of stone
Evil thoughts have graven upon,
Shade by shade and line by line,
Refashioning what was once divine.

All these sleep, and through the night,
Comes a passion and a cry,
With a blind sorrow and a might,
I know not whence, I know not why,
A something I cannot control,
A nameless hunger of the soul.
It holds me fast. In vain, in vain,
I remember how of old
I saw the ruddy race of men,
Through the glittering world outrolled,
A gay-smiling multitude,
All immortal, all divine,
Treading in a wreathèd line
By a pathway through a wood.

The Sun Cup

The earth is the cup of the sun,
That he filleth at morning with wine,
With the warm, strong wine of his might
From the vintage of gold and of light,
Fills it, and makes it divine.

And at night when his journey is done,
At the gate of his radiant hall,
He setteth his lips to the brim,
With a long last look of his eye,
And lifts it and draineth it dry,
Drains till he leaveth it all
Empty and hollow and dim.

And then, as he passes to sleep,
Still full of the feats that he did,
Long ago in Olympian wars,
He closes it down with the sweep
Of its slow-turning luminous lid,
Its cover of darkness and stars,
Wrought once by Hephæstus of old
With violet and vastness and gold.

www.ingramcontent.com/pod-product-compliance
Lightning Source LLC
Chambersburg PA
CBHW060106050426
42448CB00011B/2638